AMAZING SCIENCE

QUICKSAND

AND OTHER

EARTHLY WONDERS

Q.L. PEARCE
Illustrated by Mary Ann Fraser

Julian Messner

To Leah

Acknowledgment

With thanks to Richard Robinson, Associate Professor of Geology, Santa Monica City College (California), for his assistance and critical reading of the manuscript.

Library of Congress Cataloging-in-Publication Data
Pearce, Q.L. (Querida Lee)
  Amazing science. Quicksand and other earthly wonders / Q.L. Pearce ;
illustrated by Mary Ann Fraser.
    p. cm.
  Bibliography: p. 63
  Includes index.
  Summary: Presents "astonishing" features of our planet such as geysers,
caves, salt lakes, peat bogs, carnivorous plants, creeping swamps, and
autumn colors.
    1. Geology–Juvenile literature. 2. Geomorphology–Juvenile literature.
3. Paleontology–Juvenile literature. [1. Earth–Miscellanea. 2. Geology–
Miscellanea. 3. Curiosities and wonders.] I. Fraser, Mary Ann, ill. II. Title.
III. Title: Quicksand and other earthly wonders.
QE29.P43 1989   89-8321
508–dc20   CIP
                                                                       AC

  ISBN 0-671-68530-9 (lib. bdg.)
  ISBN 0-671-68646-1 (pbk.)

Text copyright © 1989 by RGA Publishing Group, Inc.
Illustrations copyright © 1989 by RGA Publishing Group, Inc.
All rights reserved including the right of
reproduction in whole or in part in any form.
Published by Julian Messner, a division of
Silver Burdett Press, Inc., Simon & Schuster, Inc.
Prentice Hall Bldg., Englewood Cliffs, NJ 07632.

JULIAN MESSNER and colophon are trademarks of
Simon & Schuster, Inc.
Manufactured in the United States of America.

Lib. ed.:   10 9 8 7 6 5 4 3 2 1
Paper ed.:   10 9 8 7 6 5 4 3 2 1

Contents

Our Planet Earth

We live in a very exciting time. Humans have turned their attention to the stars. We are reaching out into space, sending probes to explore the many planets of our solar system. But perhaps the most incredible planet in the solar system is right under our own feet. It is not the largest or smallest, the hottest or coldest planet, but planet Earth holds many marvels and mysteries, some that defy explanation.

Have you ever heard of a cavern seven football fields long and twenty stories high, or icy deserts where the soil is frozen solid and the trees are less than one foot tall? How about seas of singing sand, or valleys so hot and dry that rain evaporates before it reaches the ground? Did you know that there have been times when there were no ice caps on Earth at all? That the land that is now Antarctica was once a steamy jungle? Can you imagine that the enormous Sahara was once covered by vast rivers of ice?

The Earth is a constantly changing place. Even the continents, which seem so motionless and secure, are slowly floating across this planet like gigantic rafts. No matter where you look there are wonders far more exciting than fiction. From the rare to the bizarre, this book will introduce you to some peculiar and astonishing facts about our amazing planet.

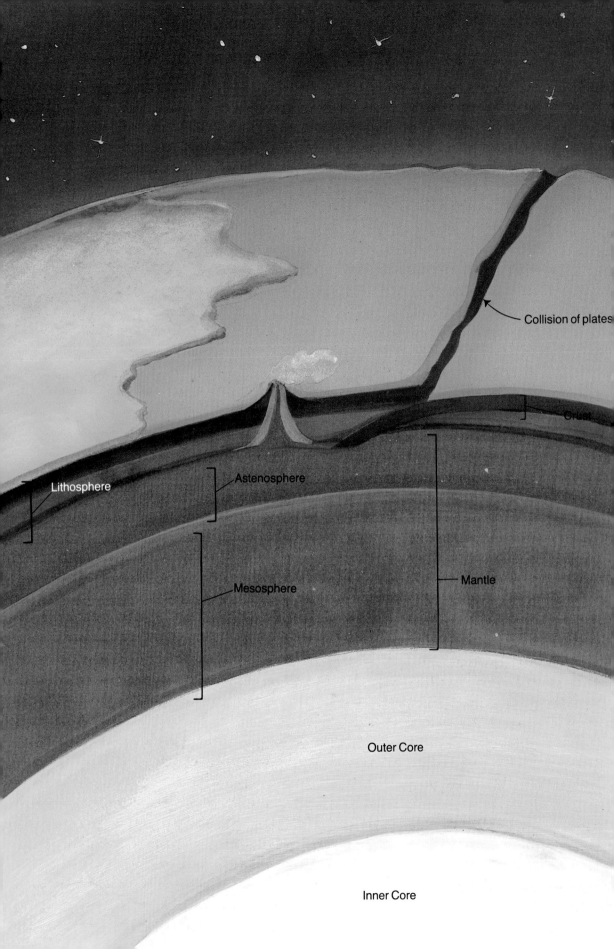

Collision of plates

Crust

Lithosphere

Astenosphere

Mantle

Mesosphere

Outer Core

Inner Core

The Center of the Earth

One of the most amazing places on our planet is actually inside of it. If our Earth were the size of an onion, the ground we are standing on would be about as thin as the onion's outer skin. In fact, our planet *is* layered like an onion. The solid crust on which we live is only five to twenty-five miles thick. But the layer below the crust, the mantle, is nearly 1,800 miles thick. The mantle is made up of molten rock that has the firmness of thick, hot fudge.

The next layer of our planet Earth is a liquid one, called the outer core. It surrounds the incredible inner core, which is a solid ball of nickel and iron. This inner core is as hot as the surface of the sun. It does not melt because of the tremendous pressure at that depth—about one billion pounds per square foot. The material that makes up the core is so dense that a single cubic foot weighs more than eight cubic feet of bricks. That's about 227 bricks!

How do we know all of these things about the inside of the Earth? You can think of it as a great mystery that was solved by following clues. Scientists learned about the Earth's interior by studying earthquakes. Earthquakes cause waves of vibration deep within the planet. Some of these waves speed through at more than five miles per second. That is eight times faster than a bullet. By studying the waves and by knowing the size and shape of the Earth, scientists figured out what is inside. Most of the million or more quakes per year are so small that we can't even feel them, but others are very powerful. The strongest earthquake in the United States shook New Madrid, Missouri, in 1811. It was so strong that it rang church bells as far away as Boston. It even caused the mighty Mississippi River to change its course.

Our amazing planet Earth is actually
layered like an onion.

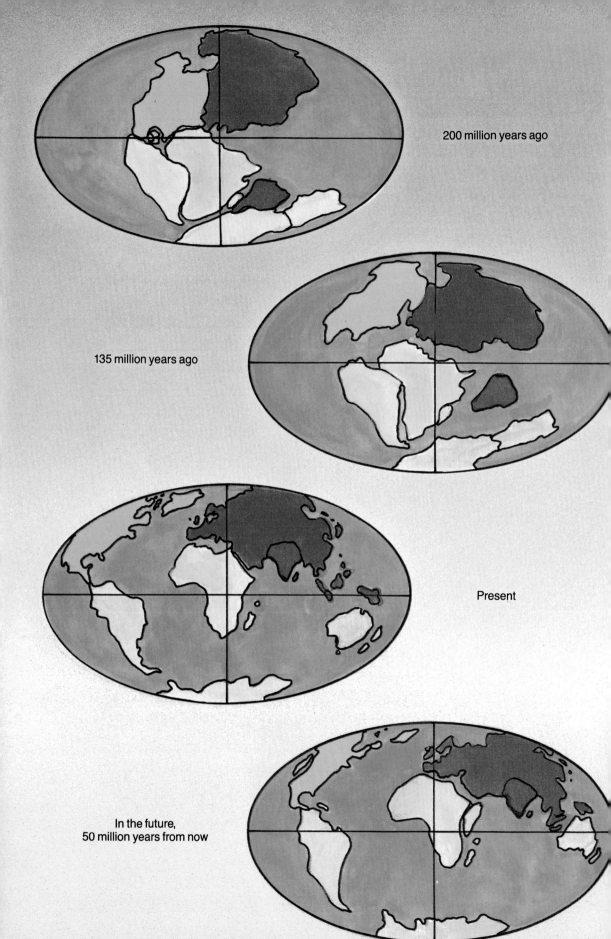

200 million years ago

135 million years ago

Present

In the future,
50 million years from now

Moving Continents

The ground beneath our feet is not as motionless as you might think. Earth's crust is cracked into huge sections called plates. These crustal plates drift slowly across the planet, carrying the continents and ocean floor with them. There are seven major plates, and they all move at different speeds. But don't worry—the fastest moves only about seven inches per year.

Because of plate movement, the continents have not always looked as they do today. At one time, they formed one immense continent called *Pangaea* (pan·GEE·uh), which is Greek for "all land." This continent was surrounded by a huge ocean called *Panthalassa* (pan·thuh·LASS·uh), or "all sea." Then great forces inside the Earth caused the land to split apart. New oceans were born in the widening gaps.

If you look at a globe, you can easily see that the coasts of South America and Africa fit together like puzzle pieces. Deep beneath the Atlantic Ocean, a gigantic mountain range follows the same outline. It is there that new ocean floor is born, and there that the South American and African plates are splitting apart. Fiery magma (molten rock from beneath the Earth's crust) squeezes up through cracks in the mountain range. It hardens into new ocean floor and moves outward, pushing the plates on either side of the ridge further apart. The Atlantic Ocean today is sixty feet wider than it was when Columbus sailed on his voyage of discovery.

Of course, when material is added to one side of a plate, it must be taken away from its other side, or the Earth's crust would have to expand like a balloon. When one plate bumps into another, it may be forced underneath, pushed down toward the mantle, and there destroyed. Earthquakes often shake the edges of the plates as they slide past each other.

In the past 200 million years, the face of planet Earth has changed dramatically.

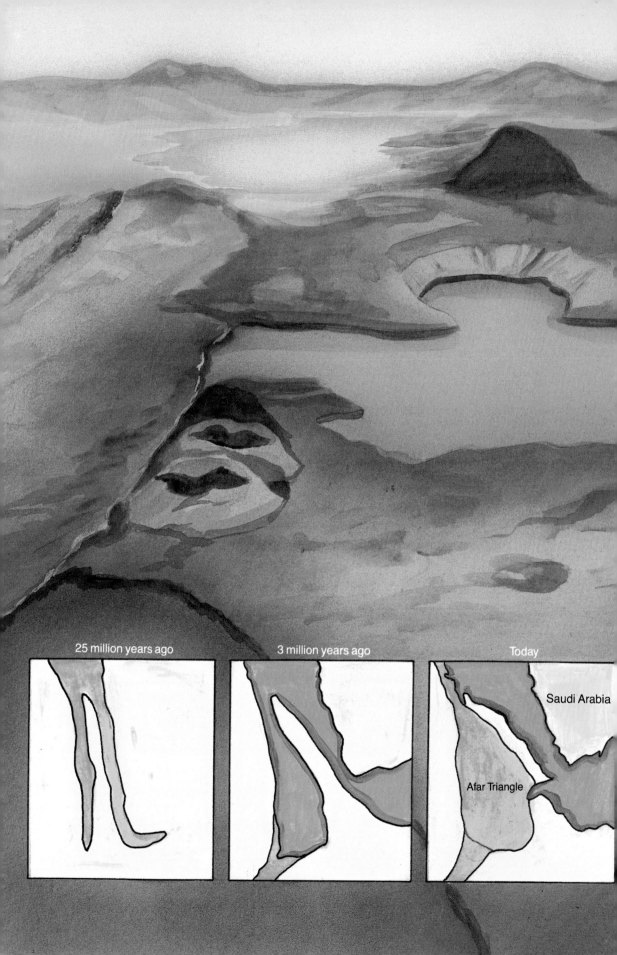

25 million years ago

3 million years ago

Today

Saudi Arabia

Afar Triangle

The Afar Triangle

There is a place in Africa where you can see the ocean's floor without getting your feet wet. Where the Arabian Peninsula moves slowly away from the African continent, a ribbon of water–the Red Sea and the Gulf of Aden–separates the two lands. The coastline of the piece that is breaking away almost perfectly matches the opposite coastline. But there is one small section where the coastlines do not fit. This low-lying triangle of land stretched across Eastern Ethiopia (ee·thee·OH·pee·uh) and Djibouti (jih·BOOT·ee) is called the Afar Triangle.

The Afar Triangle is a most peculiar place. It is actually a huge section of seafloor that has been shoved to the surface. Rock formations typical of those found on the seafloor dot the land. At one time, a hot fountain of magma pushing upward from below caused the land to bulge and crack– much the way rising steam in a baking pie causes the piecrust to bulge and crack. The great stream of molten rock produced many volcanoes and hot springs. The area is also often shaken by earthquakes.

At the northern end of the triangle lies the Danakil (DAN·uh·kil) Depression. Lying 400 feet below sea level, the flat plain looks as if it were covered by sand, but the white covering is actually salt. This salt wasteland covers 2,000 square miles, an area larger than the state of Rhode Island. The Danakil Depression was once a watery inlet of the Red Sea. When the Afar Triangle was uplifted, the inlet was cut off from its source of seawater. In the sweltering heat, the water soon evaporated, leaving behind miles of salt. Even in the winter there is no relief from the heat. Winter temperatures have been known to reach as high as 123° Fahrenheit.

The Afar Triangle–once a seafloor,
now a barren wasteland.

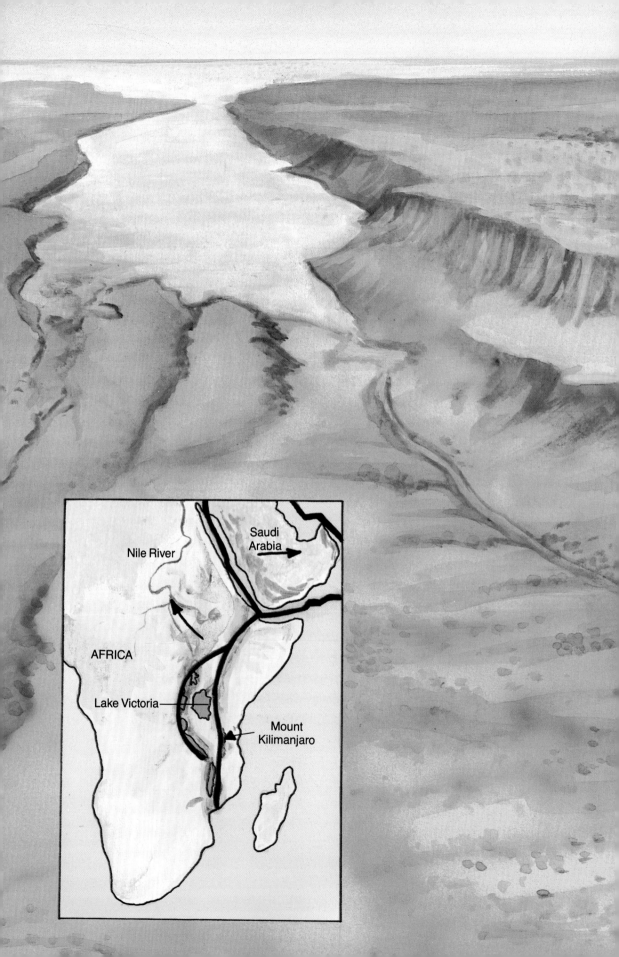

Nile River

Saudi
Arabia

AFRICA

Lake Victoria

Mount
Kilimanjaro

The Great Rift Valley

The first European explorers to reach the 1,500-mile-long Great Rift Valley of East Africa were astounded by what they saw. They could not imagine what forces could form such an unusual place. Future scientists eventually realized the explorers were witnessing the creation and spreading of new Earth crust. The Great Rift Valley is, in fact, one of the few places on dry land where you can see such a sight.

The story of the Great Rift Valley begins about twenty million years ago, when a huge mass of magma pushed its way toward the surface. The land above the rising mound of magma bulged upward and began to weaken. Eventually, the land began to split on either side of the growing mound. The splits in the land were not clean but had many ragged fractures. Between the fractures, the land collapsed and formed a huge, irregular valley from Ethiopia to Tanzania (tan·zuh·NEE·uh). Today, molten rock from beneath the Earth's crust still boils up in many places along the fractures. As new material is added, the land on either side of the valley moves slowly apart. If this continues, seawater will one day fill the valley and East Africa will be an island.

It is no surprise that the Great Rift Valley is a place of many wonders. The magma below the surface fuels two of the world's largest volcanoes, Mount Kenya and Mount Kilimanjaro (kil·uh·man·JAR·oh). One of the oddest sights is Lake Natron. This bizarre body of water is fed by volcanic hot springs. Water temperatures may reach a scalding 150° Fahrenheit. Strangely, the banks of harsh Lake Natron are home to nearly half the world's flamingos. These beautiful birds feed on the only creatures able to survive in the lake's waters: algae, insects, and brine shrimp.

*Crustal plate movement might one day
make East Africa an island.*

Floating Rocks

In 1883 in Indonesia a huge volcano called Krakatoa blew itself apart. It was one of the greatest volcanic eruptions of all time. Huge waves 120 feet high called tsunamis (soo·NAM·eez) crashed into the island of Java a little more than twenty-five miles away. Small waves even registered in the English Channel, halfway around the world. The sound of Krakatoa's explosion was heard over 3,000 miles away in the Indian Ocean. That is like an explosion in California being heard in New York. Krakatoa blew tons of ash, rock, and lava into the air, blocking out light from the sun for days. A layer of floating rock four feet thick covered the surface of the surrounding sea.

Floating rocks? Since most rocks sink, it may be hard to imagine a rock that floats. But this is pumice, and it's a very special kind of rock. A type of foamy volcanic glass, pumice is ejected from a volcano as a liquid. The liquid pumice contains a lot of gas. If it cools and hardens quickly, the escaping gases form lots of little pockets. These pockets make pumice very light—so light that you could probably lift a large chunk of this unusual rock. If the rock had cooled more slowly, the gas would not have formed pockets, and it would have become a shiny dark glass called obsidian (ub·SID·ee·un).

Pumice has some very interesting uses. The Romans used it to build waterways, called aqueducts, which still stand after 1,500 years. Surprisingly, though, pumice is very brittle, and a chunk of it may crumble if struck with force. However, the grains are also very hard, and this makes it a good abrasive material. In fact, pumice is used as an ingredient in special soap to clean very dirty hands.

The fiery explosion of Krakatoa filled the sea with floating pumice.

The Geysers of Yellowstone

In a far corner of what is now the state of Wyoming, there is a section of land that the Indians once feared. They believed it was a place of evil spirits. When explorers brought tales of this strange place to the East, people thought their stories of smoking pits, spouting pots of steam, and boiling, bubbling mud were make-believe. But eventually the area was recognized not as an evil place, but a place of beauty and many natural wonders. To preserve this natural beauty, in 1872 Yellowstone became our first national park.

The most spectacular displays of Yellowstone are incredible jets of boiling water and steam called geysers (GUY·zerz). Beneath the park, scientists discovered a "hot spot," or magma plume. This is a huge pocket of molten rock. In many places the ground is hot to the touch, even in winter. When groundwater seeps into cracks and chambers in the rock, it is heated. The chambers are often connected to a main vent that is filled with this heated water. Eventually, the water at the bottom of this "plumbing system" flashes to steam, pushing the water above it out with a roar. Sometimes just a thundering jet of volcanic gas or steam is able to escape directly to the surface. Then it is called a fumarole (FYOO·muh·role).

There are about 10,000 geysers in Yellowstone National Park. The most famous is Old Faithful. It erupts every thirty-three to ninety-four minutes. In the four to five minutes it erupts, Old Faithful shoots about 12,000 gallons of scalding hot water into the air. It is even more spectacular in winter, when the super-hot water meets the cold air, creating huge clouds of steam.

Every half hour to ninety minutes, Old Faithful shoots 12,000 gallons of steamy water into the air.

Ice Ages

Glaciers in Seattle? New York buried under hundreds of feet of ice? As strange as these may sound, they have happened and will probably happen again. Rivers of ice called glaciers (GLAY·sherz) form in the Earth's cold polar regions. As the world's climate cools or warms, glaciers spread or retreat. When they spread, it is called a glacial period. Since the Earth formed, there have been many glacial periods, or ice ages. During the last two or three million years, there have been a least four such ice ages.

At the peak of the last ice age, about 18,000 years ago, glaciers covered more than thirty percent of the land. In some places, icy glaciers two or three miles thick slid far south. As the powerful glaciers moved slowly across the land, they gouged deep scratches in rocks and moved huge boulders weighing hundreds of pounds. Ice covered half the surface of the Earth's oceans, too. So much water was frozen into ice that the sea level dropped 300 to 400 feet. This caused land bridges to appear between places that had been separated by the sea. Such a bridge formed between Alaska and Asia. Animals could walk from what we now call Siberia to Alaska without getting their feet wet.

Warmer times are called interglacials (in·ter·GLAY·shulz). We are in an interglacial period now, and only ten percent of the Earth's surface is covered by ice. Even so, we sometimes experience stages of colder-than-normal temperatures. The last of these stages took place between the 15th and 19th centuries. It was called the Little Ice Age. Glaciers in the Swiss Alps moved far down the mountains, crushing homes in their path, and the River Thames in England was frozen solid!

During the Little Ice Age, Rhone Glacier in Switzerland threatened villages.

The Arctic Tundra

Near the very top of our planet lies one of the strangest environments on Earth. Bordering the Arctic Ocean, the arctic tundra was the last area exposed when the glaciers of the last ice age withdrew about 10,000 years ago. Most tundra soil is permanently frozen as much as one mile deep. It is no wonder that scientists call this soil permafrost. In some warmer areas of the 1,000-mile-wide tundra, a few inches of the permafrost can thaw during the short summer season. It then refreezes in autumn. Though rarely more than twenty inches of rain or snow fall on the tundra each year, there are plenty of bogs, ponds, and shallow lakes. This is because the frozen ground prevents water from draining away. The water allows such animals as the snowy owl, lemming, and caribou to live comfortably on the tundra.

The strange conditions of the tundra also produce some very bizarre land formations. Because of thawing and refreezing, the ground is always shrinking or expanding. Rocks are forced up through the soil in a process called frost-heaving. In some places, large mounds of ice called pingos rise as much as 150 feet. Pingos form when pools of ground-water freeze and are forced upward. Over time, earth and grass cover the hill, but its heart is made of ice.

Have you ever seen the tall willow or birch trees of the forest? Relatives of these trees live on the arctic tundra, too. Their branches may spread out over ten or fifteen feet, but they are not the sort of trees you want to climb. These tiny trees grow only a few inches to perhaps one foot tall. The permafrost stops the tree roots from extending very deeply. This prevents the tree from obtaining the nutrients it needs to grow tall.

The bitterly cold arctic tundra is home to
the snowy owl, lemming, and caribou.

Caves and Caverns

In East Malaysia on the shores of the South China Sea, you will find Lobang Nasip Bagus, the world's largest cave. The cave is more than 2,000 feet long and 1,000 feet wide. That's long enough to fit seven football fields end to end. It is tall enough to house a twenty-story building, with room to spare.

The terms "cave" and "cavern" are often used interchangeably. Caves are a series or system of underground rooms, or chambers. There are thousands of caves in the Earth. The United States alone has 30,000, and no two are alike. Most often found in limestone rock, caves and caverns form over thousands, perhaps millions of years. Often they get their start from rain. As rainwater falls through the air, it becomes slightly acid. Much of it seeps into the ground. The acidic water dissolves part of the limestone rock, leaving behind holes and gaps. As water continues to flow or drip through, it wears away more and more rock. Soon the gaps become larger and deeper, forming cave systems.

Some of nature's most beautiful sculptures are to be found in caves, and, oddly enough, the sculptor is water. As water seeps down through the roof of the cave, it leaves a thin layer of calcium carbonate behind. Drop by drop, icicle-shaped rocks are formed. Some hang like long thin cones or spikes. These are called stalactites. The longest, free-hanging stalactite ever found is thirty-eight feet. When the water drops fall to the floor, they build cones, ledges, and stacks called stalagmites. The tallest stalagmite known is ninety-five feet tall. Sixteen tall men standing on each other's shoulders would barely reach the top of it.

Carlsbad Cavern in New Mexico—the site of some of nature's most beautiful sculptures.

Salt Lakes and Seas

Did you know that there are lakes and inland seas saltier than the ocean? Even freshwater lakes contain some mineral salts. But to be called a "salt lake," the amount of salt in the water must be at least three percent. The ocean is about 3.5 percent salt. Many lakes and inland seas also reach this level of saltiness. In fact, salt lakes take up as much of the Earth's surface area as freshwater lakes.

Salt lakes are usually found where the climate is very dry. This means not only hot deserts, but anywhere there is little yearly rain or snow. By these standards, freezing Antarctica is a special sort of desert. In fact, underneath a thirteen-foot-thick layer of antarctic ice, there is a small salt lake called Vanda. Even though it is buried under ice, the lake maintains a temperature of nearly eighty degrees Fahrenheit!

The saltiest body of water on Earth is twenty-eight percent salt. It is the Dead Sea, which lies between the countries of Israel and Jordan. The Dead Sea gets its name because animals cannot live there. Fish may enter from freshwater rivers flowing into the sea, but the salt kills them immediately. At 1,312 feet below sea level, the Dead Sea is also the lowest point on the planet.

The Great Salt Lake of Utah is the biggest, saltiest lake in the United States. It is what remains of an ancient lake named Lake Bonneville. That gigantic body of water covered 20,000 square miles (almost twice the area of Vermont) before it evaporated and left behind miles of dry salt flats. The Great Salt Lake is still slowly evaporating. Over the past 100 years, it has shrunk from 2,400 to 1,600 square miles. In a few hundred years, the Great Salt Lake may dry up completely.

When the salty water of the Dead Sea dries,
it leaves behind fantastic salt pillars.

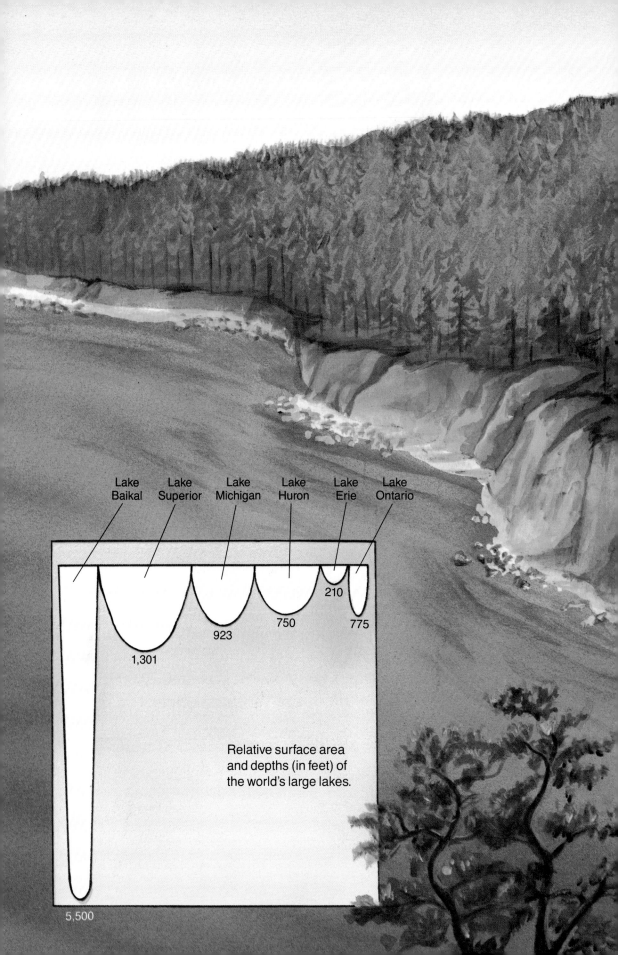

Lake
Baikal

Lake
Superior

Lake
Michigan

Lake
Huron

Lake
Erie

Lake
Ontario

210

923

750

775

1,301

Relative surface area
and depths (in feet) of
the world's large lakes.

5,500

The World's Deepest Lake

From the surface, Lake Baikal (bye·KAWL) does not look very different from any other large lake. At 395 miles long and 30 miles wide, it is a little more than one-third the surface area of Lake Superior. But Lake Baikal in Russia is nearly a mile deep, or three times as deep as Lake Superior. In fact, it holds more water than all of the Great Lakes combined.

The reason Lake Baikal is so deep is that it is actually a great opening, or rift, in the Earth's crust that over time has filled with water. Eighty million years ago, when *Tyrannosaurus rex* still roamed the Earth, the land that was to become Lake Baikal split apart, leaving behind a great wedge of space. About twenty-five million years ago, the rift began to slowly fill with rainwater and melting snow.

Hundreds of different animals and plants live in this unique place. A freshwater seal called the nerpa is found nowhere else on Earth. There is also a fish that "cries out" when caught. Called the omul, you know when you have hooked one because it lets out a sharp cry as it leaves the water. This sound is actually air escaping from its swim bladder (a gas-filled sac that helps the fish to stay at a particular depth). The largest fish in the lake is the sturgeon. It may grow as long as ten feet and weigh 500 pounds. The eggs of this fish are sold as the delicacy caviar (CAV·ee·ar).

Probably the strangest fish of all is the golomyanka (go·lum·YAN·kuh). At least one-third of this fish's body weight is made up of oil. It prefers colder, deeper waters and surfaces to feed only at night. In fact, water much warmer than forty-five degrees may be deadly for this odd creature. When their bodies wash up on shore, the sunlight melts their fat completely away, leaving very little behind.

At 5,500 feet deep, Lake Baikal is deeper than all the Great Lakes combined.

carbon dioxide gas

Lake Nyos

Village

White dots are carbon dioxide

The Exploding Lake

People living in a valley near Lake Nyos in West Africa whisper fearful tales of evil spirits that live in the lake. They claim that at times the spirits become very angry and kill the people of the valley. Evil spirits were not the cause, but on August 21, 1986, this peaceful lake was responsible for the death of 1,700 people.

The trouble began in the early evening. With a low rumbling sound, the waters of Lake Nyos began to quiver. Suddenly, a blast of wind that smelled like rotten eggs rushed upwards from the lake. A strange cloud then gushed from the water and swooped down on the small village of Lower Nyos in the valley below the lake. The 150-foot-high cloud flowed over the sleepy village. Within moments everyone was dead and the fields were covered with lifeless cattle. It was as if a bomb had exploded, which is not far from the truth.

For a long time before the lake "exploded," a colorless gas called carbon dioxide was seeping into the water. This gas probably came from beneath the lake bottom. The gas was held down near the bottom by the weight of the water above it. Scientists do not agree on what actually set the blast off. It could have been a landslide or a tiny earthquake. Whatever it was, the deadly gas exploded upward and spilled into the valley. Carbon dioxide, the same gas used to make soft drinks bubbly, is heavier than the air we breathe. When the cloud of carbon dioxide from Lake Nyos sank over the village, it pushed the air away. The people and animals suffocated.

Now Lake Nyos is peaceful once more, but the people who live in the valley still talk of evil spirits sleeping in the water. They hope that they do not wake again.

Peaceful Lake Nyos was a time
bomb waiting to explode.

Quicksand

You may not have thought of it like this before, but you can hold the world in a handful of sand. A handful of sand contains thousands of tiny grains from such objects as mighty boulders, chunks of volcanic rock, huge coral reefs, or even delicate seashells. Over decades, even centuries, wind, waves, and weather erode these objects away bit by bit, forming vast deserts or windswept beaches.

One of the most well-known types of sand is quicksand. Unlike the imaginary quicksand of movies, true quicksand is simply a bed of smooth-grained sand that becomes saturated with water. When loose sand is dry, it is fairly firm under your feet. When wet, like sand at the beach, you may find it gives way more easily and you sink a little deeper. When enough water is added, perhaps from underground springs, the loose sand becomes almost fluid. This is known as quicksand. In movies, quicksand sucks a victim down. In reality, quicksand is very dense and most people can float on it.

Sinking sand is one thing, but what is singing sand? In the desert, if the day has been windy, but the evening is still, hills of desert sand may sometimes sound a low-pitched note that will last for several minutes. On his journey to the East, the famous traveler Marco Polo wrote about the singing sand. He said it sounded like beating drums. No one is sure why the sand sings, but research has shown that the higher the temperature of the sand the louder the sound. While desert sands boom, beach sands whistle. On beaches on America's East Coast, you can cause a low-pitched whistle by quickly pushing a stick into the sand.

Underground springs turn ordinary sand into dangerous quicksand.

Shifting Sands

Waves are found not only on the ocean. Giant waves of sand called dunes move slowly across many of Earth's great deserts. There are many different kinds of dunes. The type that forms depends on the sort of sand available and the direction and strength of the wind. A dune forms when blowing sand builds up behind something in the path of the wind, like a boulder. As the pile of sand grows, it, too, becomes an obstacle to the wind, and the pile grows still higher.

The difficulty in studying sand dunes is that they don't stay put. Some creep along between 30 and 150 feet or more a year. If the wind blows steadily in one direction, the sand grains are carried up one side of the dune to the top. This process is called saltation, which means "to jump." The grains then fall over and down the front slope of the dune, or the slip face. Here, there is less wind. Sand is always being moved away from the back slope of the dune and added to the slip face. In this way the huge mound moves slowly forward.

The highest sand dunes in the United States are found at Great Sand Dunes National Monument in Colorado. They may swell to 700 feet in height. There are even bigger dunes in the Sahara (which, by the way, in Arabic means "desert") that can reach 1,000 feet high and are many miles long. Truly gigantic dunes are called draas. That is an Arabic word used to describe a great mountain of sand. Draas can soar as high as 1,600 feet. That's taller than the Empire State Building. The draas make up a vast sea of sand, called an erg. The world's largest erg is on the Arabian Peninsula. It is a patch of sand about 700 miles long and 400 miles wide called *Rub'al Khali* (ROB·uh'el HALL·ee), or "the Empty Quarter."

In a matter of months, gigantic sand dunes could cover these palm trees.

33

Death Valley

Above the floor of Death Valley in California is a 6,000-foot peak called Dante's View. From the top of this peak, you can take in an astounding sight: Looking west, you will see not only the highest point in the lower forty-eight states, but also the lowest point in the United States. Mount Whitney soars to 14,494 feet above sea level, and Badwater, in Death Valley National Monument, is 282 feet below sea level.

Death Valley is not only the lowest place in the United States, but also the hottest and driest. True to its name, it is not a place you'd want to visit in the summer. Walking across the valley on a very hot day probably feels like walking on a frying pan. Summertime temperatures regularly reach 120° Fahrenheit and have been recorded as high as 134°. The ground may be 50° hotter than the air above it. Very little cooling rain falls here, and when it does, it often evaporates before hitting the ground.

Death Valley has not always been dry. During the last ice age, it was covered by an icy cold lake that was more than 500 feet deep. Now most of the water in the valley is in salt ponds, marshes, and a few freshwater pools. One of the desert's rarest inhabitants is the Devil's Hole pupfish. This amazing fish is well adapted to the desert and can survive in water temperatures as hot as 122° Fahrenheit.

There are many unsolved mysteries about this strange valley. Perhaps one of the oddest is the valley's "moving rocks." Huge rocks, sometimes weighing one hundred pounds or more, move great distances across the valley floor. They must slide across the flat lake bed because they leave deep trails behind them. Some people think it is the wind that pushes the boulders, but the truth remains a mystery.

Badwater—the lowest point in the United States— is a land of harsh beauty.

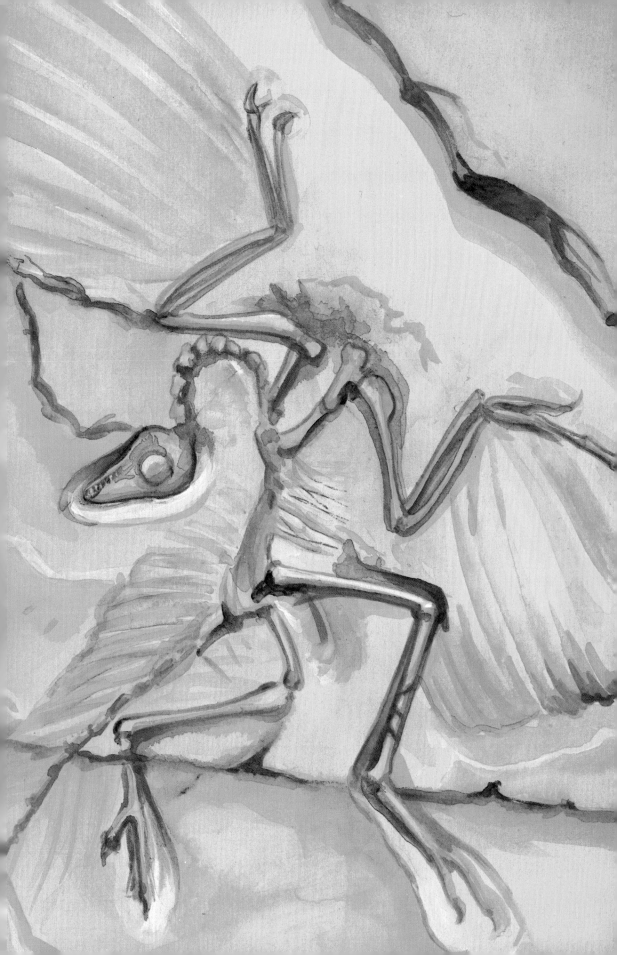

History in Stone

Do you have a favorite dinosaur? Perhaps it is the huge brontosaurus or scary tyrannosaurus. Have you ever wondered how we know what they looked like and how they lived? The answers are captured in stone. Trapped in Earth's rocks are fossils, the remains or traces of ancient plants and animals. Fossils may be anything from bones or teeth to animal droppings, footprints, or even grains of plant pollen.

It is very fortunate that fossils form at all. Conditions have to be just right. To become fossilized, a creature has to be buried quickly, perhaps in the mud at the bottom of a lake. Over many years, the mud then hardens into stone, with its valuable secret locked inside. Usually the soft parts of the animal decay. Hard parts such as bones and teeth may be preserved in their original state. Sometimes they are changed by a process called petrification (pet·rih·fih·KAY·shun). This happens when water seeping into the stone dissolves the animal remains and replaces them with minerals in the water. Exposed to wind and weather, the rock slowly wears away, and finally the fossil remains are uncovered. With luck, the fossil will be in a place where humans can find it. As you can see, there is a lot of good fortune involved.

There are other ways that remains can be preserved. In dry desert areas, some animals simply dry out after they die. In such rare cases, scientists have found bits of skin and even the stomach contents of these "mummies." Many prehistoric insects were trapped in amber. Amber is ancient, hardened tree sap. One large piece that was found holds a spider stalking another insect. Something happened to trap both insects in the sticky sap, and there they have remained for millions of years.

The ancient remains of an archaeopteryx
can be found in fossilized stone.

The La Brea Tar Pits

In the middle of Los Angeles, an imperial mammoth, an ancient relative of the elephant, battles for its life. It is in the center of a large black lake of tar, a thick, dark, sticky fluid. Near the mammoth are other fantastic creatures from the past, such as the giant ground sloth and the saber-toothed cat. These are only statues, but the bones of the animals they represent have been taken from the very area where the statues now stand.

In 1769, the Spanish explorer Gaspar de Portola was making his way slowly northward from Mexico to Monterey. As he passed through the area that is now Los Angeles, he found what appeared to be thick pools of tar seeping up from the ground. The first non-Indian to discover the pits, he called the area Rancho La Brea. *Brea* is Spanish for tar. The Indians were well aware of the pools and used the sticky black goo to seal their canoes and waterproof their baskets.

In 1901, a crew of men was searching for oil on the site. While drilling a well, the workers found some strange bones. The bones were given to the famous scientist W. W. Orcutt. He saw right away that this was an important archaeological discovery. These bones were the remains of creatures that had walked the Earth 10,000 years before. The tar had kept the bones from crumbling away. Since then, the bones of 200 different animal species have been been discovered. Even one human skeleton has been found.

How did the animals get into the tar? Probably the tar pits were covered with a layer of water. When animals came to drink, they became forever stuck in the sticky mass. The giant animals that once roamed the land are gone now. But their story is there, preserved in the tar.

*An imperial mammoth fights for its
life in a pit of deadly, black tar.*

Peat Bogs

Did you know that coal comes from plants? Today's coal comes from huge swamps and bogs that existed nearly 300,000,000 years ago. The coal-making process begins when leaves, stems, and other plant matter fall into a body of water. The material forms layers beneath the surface. As each layer thickens, it gets heavier and presses down on the layers below. Eventually, it becomes a solid mass. This mass is called peat (PEET). Peat is the first stage of the formation of coal.

A peat bog is the place where peat is formed, and it is very much like a swamp. The difference is that swamps are dominated by trees, while bogs are dominated by moss. The most common moss is called sphagnum. This ground-hugging plant can absorb a lot of water. Indians who lived near bogs in Maine used it to diaper their babies. Peat, too, has many uses. When dried, it can be burned like logs. Peat products are used to clean up oil spills in the ocean.

Like swamps, peat bogs can seem mysterious, even spooky. Many centuries ago, some societies buried their dead in the bogs. Perhaps they realized the bogs were actually a good place for burial. That's because the water in a peat bog is slightly acidic and contains little oxygen. These prevent the growth of bacteria that would cause a body to decay. In Manchester, England, men working in a bog made a grisly discovery—the well-preserved body of a man. To the amazement of the scientists who examined the man, he turned out to be more than 2,000 years old. It appeared he had been murdered. His skull was cracked and his back broken. Known as the Lindow Man, he is the most famous find, but at least 2,000 other bodies have been removed from peat bogs around the world.

Dried bricks of peat can be used for fuel.

Meat-Eating Plants

Many people are vegetarians. That means they eat only plants. But have you ever heard of a plant that eats only meat? A number of plants, in fact, survive by trapping and eating insects. They are usually found in swampy areas or bogs. Most plants get life-giving nitrogen from the soil, but the soils of swamps lack nitrogen. There is, however, nitrogen in the bodies of insects and other small creatures, and that is where these plants manage to find it. Since plants obviously cannot hunt their prey, they must trap it.

The most beautiful of the meat-eating plants is probably the sundew. There are many different kinds of sundews, each with leaves, or "traps," of different size and shape. But no matter what shape, stiff short hairs grow from the sundews leaves. Each hair is tipped with a drop of sticky liquid. The liquid glistens in the sun, attracting curious insects that become stuck in the sticky fluid. In Africa, where sundews grow to be huge, the plant's two-foot-long leaves are known to trap even mice.

The Venus' flytrap is found only in the swamps of North and South Carolina. Each leaf appears to be folded in half. When open, the sweet-smelling, reddish center attracts insects. Once an insect lands, however, the leaf slams shut and the creature is trapped in a deadly prison. Soon the plant's juices dissolve and absorb the edible parts of the insect. Each trap may be used about three times before it withers and dies.

The common pitcher plant uses a different tactic. At the base of each of its slender, pitcher-shaped leaves is a pool of fluid. A visiting insect crawls inside the pitcher, slides on the slippery walls, and falls into the liquid where it drowns.

The lovely but meat-eating pitcher plant— dangerous to careless insects.

Seeds on the Move

No one would plant weeds in their garden. So, how do they get there? They travel. In fact, plant seeds can float, glide, and hitchhike great distances. For example, the coconut, probably the world's largest seed, may roll and float a long way from the parent plant. Most seeds cannot survive in salt water, but the coconut has a hard covering that keeps out the salt water. It can survive a journey of several thousand miles across an ocean. This is one way that plants establish themselves on islands.

The winds are filled with seeds. Perhaps you have even helped to send some on their way by blowing on a fluffy dandelion and making a wish. Dandelion seeds are at one end of long spikes. At the other end soft, fluffy "parachutes" open and carry the tiny seed away on the breeze.

Animals may also carry seeds. They stick to the animals' fur and are carried away from the parent plant. When finally dropped, the seeds will grow when the weather and soil conditions are just right.

Sometimes conditions are not good and seeds don't grow right away. Perhaps they must wait for the rainy season or for the days to become sunny and warm. This is usually not too long, but sometimes seeds can wait years before growing. The record for the longest wait was set by some seeds found in the frozen soil of Alaska. They had been stored by tiny mammals in their burrows and then frozen in the ground. Scientists were surprised to discover that the seeds were at least 10,000 years old. They were even more surprised when they planted them. Several plants grew and blossomed into lovely lavender flowers. Those seeds had waited 100 centuries to bloom.

A coconut seed can survive a 1,000-mile
ocean journey before washing ashore.

The World's Largest Flower

On the jungle islands of Java and Sumatra, the climate is hot and wet all year long. At certain times of the year, ten or even twenty inches of rain may fall in twenty-four hours. Here you will find more kinds of plant and animal life than anywhere else on Earth. If you are lucky, in the steamy shadows you will also find one of the rarest, certainly the largest, of flowers in the world—the rafflesia.

On the jungle floor there is very little light. Only about two percent of the sunlight falling on the trees above filters through the dense leafy cover to reach the floor. For this reason, the rafflesia is a parasite, which means it gets its food and water by living on another plant, called its "host." In fact, the rafflesia doesn't bother with soil and lives almost entirely hidden between the wood and the bark of its vine host. Only the huge flower is visible. This strange plant has no need of green leaves, either. The rafflesia blooms quietly on the darkened jungle floor, while the host vine that feeds it gathers sunlight far overhead in the jungle canopy.

The rafflesia grows from tiny, sticky seeds carried to the host vine by small animals or ants. Soon the seeds send out thin threads that wrap around the host but do not harm it. About eighteen months later, a two-inch-wide bud begins to bulge through the bark of the vine. Within four days a huge flower blossoms. It has five leathery, rust-colored petals covered with swollen white spots. This gigantic red flower can be up to three feet across and may weigh fifteen pounds. It's not likely you'd find the rafflesia at your local florist. Unfortunately, it produces an unpleasant scent to attract the flies that pollinate it. Nicknamed the "stinking corpse lily," this amazing flower smells like rotting meat.

The giant flower rafflesia lives on the
dark, steamy floor of the jungle.

Plants Without Soil

Have you ever noticed sprigs of mistletoe fastened over a doorway during the Christmas season? Because mistletoe doesn't need soil to survive, ancient Europeans thought it was an evil plant with strange magical powers. That is not true, but the mistletoe does have a bad side. It is a parasite, which means it lives off another plant, called the host. It may even cause the host plant to die. A typical plant has roots that reach into the soil. The roots anchor the plant and absorb water and nutrients. The mistletoe, however, sends its roots deep into the branches of host trees. There is even a kind of mistletoe that grows on other mistletoe.

Not all plants that grow without soil are parasites. Epiphytes, sometimes called "air plants," live in trees. This large group of plants, which includes many varieties of orchids, ferns, bromeliads, and mosses, takes nothing but support from the host. The roots anchor the plant to the tree. Epiphytes often grow in the "V" made by a tree's strong main branches. Some collect their own soil by capturing rotting leaves in a tangled root basket. Since they can't draw water from the soil, many epiphytes rely on the rains for water.

Bromeliads, a type of epiphyte, actually trap the water they need. The center of the plants' tightly fitted leaves forms a cup that collects water in a pool. This little pool also makes the tree-dwelling plant an attractive home for many tiny creatures. Certain insects such as mosquitoes and dragonflies feed and lay their eggs in the pool. Tiny frogs, salamanders, and spiders then come to feed on the insects. The bromeliad's colorful, sweet-smelling flowers attract, and are often pollinated by, one of the wonders of the bird world –the tiny, incredible hummingbird.

*Living high on tree branches, these exotic
air plants don't need soil to survive.*

The Baobab Tree

There is an old African legend that one day a devil in anger pulled a baobab (BAH·oh·bab) tree from the ground. He shoved it back upside down, and it has grown that way ever since. The baobab's fantastic shape is indeed unmistakable: This odd African tree looks as if it were growing upside down. Its huge tangled branches look more like roots. Furthermore, the branches often spread out so far that the tree is as wide as it is tall. The baobab's width, in fact, is all out of proportion to its height. The trunk alone may be up to thirty feet wide on a fifty-foot-tall tree.

Despite its strangeness, the baobab is a well-adapted tree. On the African savannah (suh·VAN·uh) where the trees are found, the climate is often hot and dry for long periods. These trees do not mind, however, because they can hold water very well. In dry years, the trees may grow very slowly or not at all. In very dry years, large trees may even shrink. These amazing trees are so well suited to their harsh surroundings that if all goes well, they may live to 1,000 years of age.

The baobab is also useful in many ways. It provides a lightweight timber. Local inhabitants use the spongy, pinkish bark to make rope and cloth. The standing baobab also produces a sweet fruit that is a very good source of vitamin C, and its flowers provide a tasty meal for nocturnal, nectar-eating bats. But that's not all this huge tree provides. Would you believe that natives of Kenya have been known to hollow out old trees and live inside? The hollow baobab trunk makes a very good home and also provides an excellent "tank" to catch and store rainwater.

The fantastic baobab tree—wide enough
for a family to hollow out and live in.

Saguaro Cactus

Remember western movies that end with a cowboy riding off into the sunset? The desert scene wouldn't be complete without the saguaro (suh·WAR·uh) cactus. These tall plants are found only in Mexico and the southwestern United States. Although they are often pictured with only two arms, they may have as many as five or six or none at all.

The saguaro is slow-growing. In its first ten years, it only grows between one and five inches. But a fully grown plant of fifty to seventy years may get as tall as fifty feet and weigh up to ten tons. That's heavier than an elephant. The saguaro often lives to a ripe old age of 150 to 200 years.

Like most cactus, the saguaro lives in the hot, dry desert, where it is important to be able to find and conserve water. This spiny cactus has developed ways of doing both. Its strong, shallow, widespread roots soak up the slight desert rain. A very big saguaro can soak up enough water to fill three bathtubs, or more than 1,500 gallons. It stores this water in the pulpy tissue in its stem. Ridges all around the stem allow it to expand when full of water. The cactus may actually swell to twice its normal size.

The saguaro is sometimes called "the desert's high-rise apartments." A red-tailed hawk may build a nest in one of its arms. The Gila woodpecker builds its gourd-shaped nest in the large main stem, which the cactus seals with a corky substance. The stem makes a perfect nest because the air inside can be twenty-five degrees cooler than the outside air during the day, and at night it can be twelve degrees warmer. When the woodpeckers leave, the nest is often taken over by elf owls, the world's smallest owls.

The saguaro cactus should be called "the desert's high-rise apartments."

The Colors of Autumn

Nature's most colorful display takes place in North America in the fall. The air is crisp and cool, and the forests seem painted with patches of gold, purple, fiery red, and orange.

Most leaves are green because they contain a green material called chlorophyll (KLOR·uh·fill). That is a special substance that helps them to turn sunlight and water into food. This food-making process is called photosynthesis (foh·toh·SIN·thuh·sis). In autumn, this process slows down. Each leaf then produces a special growth of cells at the base of the stalk. These cells cut off the water supply that the leaf needs to keep producing chlorophyll. Since no more chlorophyll is being produced, the green color fades, and the leaf's true color appears.

Leaves are generally yellow, but other factors produce different colors. Acid and sugar bring out red. That is why sugar maple leaves are so crimson. When a leaf's inner layer of yellow shines through an outer layer of red, we see fiery red-orange. But these beautiful autumn colors do not last for long, perhaps only several weeks. The stem soon becomes weak. A light wind can pull the leaf away, or it may just fall when it can no longer support its own weight. Trees that change color and drop their leaves in this way are called deciduous (dih·SIJ·uh·wus).

At one time people thought frost brought on this change. Actually, early frost kills the leaves before the colorful change can take place. Well-fertilized soils may keep leaves so green that the frost kills them before they die off naturally. For that reason, trees that grow in areas where the soil is poor usually put on a more colorful show.

Nature puts on a dazzling display
of color every autumn.

Ant Farmers

As incredible as it may sound, certain types of ants actually raise their own food. Weaver ants are fierce fighters and usually prey on other insects for food, but they are also like tiny dairy farmers. High in the treetops, they keep herds of smaller insects such as pale green or brown aphids (also known as "ant cows"). While the tiny aphids suck the sap from plant stems, the ferocious weaver ants protect the herd from birds and other enemies. The ants may even build leafy tents over their herd. The smallest of the worker ants cleans and strokes the insect "cattle." This encourages the aphids to give off a sweet liquid called honeydew, which the ants then use as food.

There is another kind of ant that raises a crop of fungus. This is the leaf-cutter ant of the Central and South American rain forests. Leaf-cutter ants have very sharp mouthparts, with edges shaped like a steak knife. They use these special tools to clip ragged pieces from green leaves. A large colony of leaf-cutter ants can strip a small tree bare overnight.

Once the leaf-cutter ants have clipped their leafy prize, they travel in a long procession back to the nest. This may be a distance of one hundred yards or more. That's about the length of a football field–a far distance for tiny ants to travel. The leaves are then carried to chambers ten to eighteen feet deep within the underground nest. Here, one group of workers chews the leaves until they are mushy, then mixes them with saliva and waste matter. This sticky paste is food for a special kind of fungus that grows only in these underground chambers. The fungus is food for the ants. When a new queen ant leaves the colony to start her own nest, she always carries a small bit of fungus to start her own garden.

Leaf-cutter ant farmers carry
their "harvest" back to the nest.

Spider Silk

Almost anywhere you go on Earth you will find spiders, and most produce threads of silk. These threads are very strong and flexible. A single strand can hold five times more weight than an identical strand of steel. A spider thread thinner than a human hair can be stretched to twice its length before breaking. There are different kinds of silk for different jobs. Most spiders can spin several kinds, depending on the job to be done.

Spiders are among the few insects that make traps to catch food. Several kinds of silk (dry, sticky, or woolly) may be used to make the special trap known as the web. Each kind of spider spins a particular kind of web. Some are quite beautiful. Others look very untidy and irregular. Another type of silk is used to wrap a spider's prey, which sometimes will be stored and eaten later. The strongest silk is for the drag line, a "safety line" that the spider can produce very quickly. When threatened, the spider hangs from the drag line and rapidly lowers itself to a safer spot.

Spiders may be the original hang gliders. When ready to leave home, a young spiderling stands on its head and tosses a long, dry strand of silk to the wind. This "ballooning silk" lifts it into the air. The spiderling may float for great distances. At times the sky is filled with these lines, also called gossamer, drifting in the breeze.

Another kind of very fine silk is produced by the female spider to make a protective case for her eggs. It is so fine that in the 18th century, Parisians used the silk to make gloves and stockings.

The silken, sticky web of the spider catches dinner very handily.

Human-Made Mysteries

Do you like a good mystery? On a tiny island in the South Pacific lies one of humankind's most bewildering puzzles. The island is Easter Island, named for the day on which it was discovered.

In this lonely place are hundreds of gigantic stone statues. The peculiar statues, which all face toward the ocean, are called moai. Each has the same long ears, squared chin, and rounded belly. Many are between twelve and fifteen feet tall and weigh twenty tons. The largest is thirty-two feet tall and weighs ninety tons, heavier than a passenger car on a train.

It's astonishing that these giants were carved, but the biggest mystery is how they were moved. There are many ideas about this. Evidence has been found of a system of cords, cables, and rollers that may have been used. Unfortunately, there is no one left to tell us, and the statues only stare silently out to sea.

An island on the other side of the world holds another strange puzzle. On a quiet plain in the south of England stands Stonehenge, a mysterious double ring of enormous gray stones. These stones were shaped and placed there almost 4,000 years ago. Many of the building stones, called bluestones, weigh four tons each and were brought from mountains in Wales 240 miles away. That would be like dragging a truck from New York City to Boston.

Exactly how and why Stonehenge was built we may never know. The position of the stones seems to have something to do with the movements of the sun, moon, and stars. Perhaps it was a temple, or an ancient observatory, or both.

The massive rocks of Stonehenge and Easter Island—mysteries locked within the past.

The Future of Our Planet Earth

The Earth holds many wonders, and it seems that every day an astonishing discovery is added to the list. Still, the greatest marvel of our Earth is how everything is in balance. All the different environments—the desert and tundra, the forest and swamp, the seashore and mountaintop—are delicately linked. What affects one affects them all. Humans have been on Earth a relatively short time, but they have already made many changes. Some are not very good.

The rainforests are being cleared for timber or to create more farmland. Africa has already lost half of its forests, and the rest could be gone in thirty years. In their search for oil, humans are disrupting the fragile environments of the tundra and the seashore. As humankind drains the swamps and bogs, it destroys the habitats of the plants and animals that live there.

There have been good changes, too. By understanding our Earth, we are learning to work with the environment and not against it. New methods have been developed for soil conservation. The habitats of certain plants and animals are now being carefully protected. Some endangered species are even making a comeback. In many cases, the use of natural resources is more carefully planned. There is still plenty for us to do, however. By working together we can be sure that future generations, too, may marvel at the wonders of our incredible Earth.

For Further Reading

Bresler, Lynn: *Earth Facts,* Tulsa, Oklahoma, EDC Publishing, 1986.

Holmes, Anita: *Cactus, the All-American Plant,* New York City, Four Winds Press, 1982.

Knight, David: *The First Book of Deserts,* New York City, Franklin Watts, Inc., 1964.

Lauber, Patricia: *Seeds Pop-Stick-Glide,* New York City, Crown Publishers, 1981.

Lerner, Carol: *Pitcher Plants, the Elegant Insect Traps,* New York City, William Morrow and Co., 1983.

Lougee, Laura: *The Web of the Spider,* Bloomfield Hills, Michigan, Cranbrook Institute of Science, 1964.

Overbeck, Cynthia: *Carnivorous Plants,* Minneapolis, Minnesota, Lerner Publications, 1982.

Seddon, Tony, and Baily, Jill: *The Living World,* Garden City, New York, Doubleday & Co., 1986.

Index